Tho

Book of

Home Truths

Thora Hird's Book of Home Truths

Dame Thora Hird, OBE

with Liz Barr

HarperCollins*Publishers*

HarperCollins*Publishers*
77–85 Fulham Palace Road, London w6 8jb

First published in Great Britain in 1994
by HarperCollins*Religious*

This edition 1998

3 5 7 9 10 8 6 4 2

A catalogue record for this book
is available from the British Library

isbn 000 628066 8

Printed and bound in Great Britain by
Woolnough Bookbinding Ltd,
Irthlingborough, Northamptonshire

Contents

Dedicated to
'THE ONE WHO KNOWS',
AND TO THE GREAT PEOPLE
OF LANCASHIRE

Introduction

Do you remember the 'Household Tips'
they used to give in Women's magazines
and journals? No, not the sort of thing you
see on the covers of magazines today …
honestly, I don't know where to look
sometimes … I'll be searching through the
station bookstall for something light to
read on the train, and find myself transfixed
by: 'Curing Impotence with an Electric

Blanket' or 'Sex and the over Sixties ...'.

But, as I was saying, in the forties and fifties – well, you may be too young to remember, but I'm not – women's magazines would have more creative ambitions. For instance, an interesting little feature might be entitled: 'How to use soap to stop your drawers from sticking' or 'How to Conduct a Soirée for Six in your New Flatlet'. These 'household tips' – and this is the best part – were nearly always written by (Drum-roll) ... 'One Who Knows'!

I wonder whatever became of 'One Who Knows'. We could do with some of her 'household tips' today: 'How to Open the Seven Layers of Plastic Wrapping round Everything You Buy in the Supermarket Without Breaking your Nails and Spilling the Lot on the Floor' for a start.

Now God's listening, I've never thought of myself as 'One Who Knows', or even as someone who could or should be telling anybody (other than my own nearest and dearest, that is) what's what. I hope nobody has ever said 'Thora's a right know-all!' But it was remembering 'One Who Knows' that gave me an idea for this book.

I left school at fourteen, so you might know, I've never been to university, like some of you clever-heads … **but** I have got a degree – Doctor of Literature, no less!

As Scottie and Jan accompanied me to the Graduation Hall in Lancaster to receive my honorary degree, about eight years ago now it must have been, I must admit to feeling rather proud of myself, thinking of

how Princess Alexandra, Chancellor of
the University, would be doing the
presentation, and wishing my mother and
father could have been there to see it. Then,
as we were driving along, very nearly there,
I suddenly went 'Heeee-aaaaah!'

Well, that's the closest I can get to writing
out the noise I made – a long intake of
breath expressing surprise, shock, delight
and a flood of memories – all brought on
by seeing a place I recognized and hadn't
seen for over fifty years: the Ashton Hall,
Lancaster.

The Lancaster and District Co-op, where
I worked as a cashier for ten years, held an
annual Dinner and Dance in the Ashton
Hall each year. Tickets were half-a-crown
(12½p) (including dinner). The first time

I went, I thought I had better have a new ballgown (get that bit – *ballgown* – and did you notice *new* – as though it was the latest in a long line?!) So I went to Doris Brown's, who lived further down our street, and asked her advice. As usual, she was most helpful, and said she would make me one.

It was in *eau-de-nil* satin, low-waisted, with a skirt that had four handkerchief points, and about a ten-inch deep piece of georgette round the bottom. I hope you can visualize it – sounds 'orrible, doesn't it? But really, it was quite pretty. I wore real silk stockings and brocade evening shoes in pale pink and green (*eau-de-nil*), white gloves, and a little evening bag with a lace-edged hanky in it, a mirror, a lipstick, and my ticket and a half-a-crown (in case I needed any money apart from my bus fare – sixpence to go and sixpence to return home – and that's 6d, kindly note, not 6p!)

When my best friend, Peg, and I arrived, people were being seated for dinner, so we took our places. I will now tell you exactly what happened. A band was playing popular music – 'Horsey, Keep Your Tail Up' or some such suitable number. Peg and I were very excited and happy, and expecting an enjoyable evening. The soup (cream of mushroom) was served, and lots of laughing and jolly chat was taking place. As the waiter started to put a plate of soup in front of me, he caught his elbow on the chair-back of the person next to me … Yes, you've guessed it. The entire portion of soup tipped straight into my lap! It was very hot, and went right through the dress and real silk stockings. I let out a yell, jumped up and Peg rushed after me into the Ladies' Room.

Now I know we speak of 'the Good Old Days' but in one respect, 'Ladies' Room-wise', they weren't half as good as they are now … I mean, no little piles of towels or machines blowing out hot air – nothing. Well, there was a 'roller towel' behind the door (remember them?), but it was so high up, we could only reach the bottom two inches, both being little 'uns, and as for trying to wipe my dress with it, even jumping up and down, well – it was impossible. If only 'One Who Knows' had been on hand – she'd have known what to do!

We pulled my dress off to rinse the soup off the front, disarranging my hair, which was in fashionable 'earphones' – y'know, plaits wound round like saucers. By now the tears were very near, the front of my dress was dripping wet – more or less free of soup, I'll admit, but dripping wet. We did the best we could with our two little lace-edged hankies, tidied my hair and bravely went back to our dinner places. You'll appreciate that dinner was nearly over by now. Everyone was very sympathetic, of course ... but that's not it, is it? Soon the dancing started, and a young fellow came up and asked if he could 'have the pleasure' of this dance. I said: 'No! I can't dance with a wet frock.'

As sharp as a knife, he answered 'I'm not

a wet frock!' A real comic (I don't think).
He said that if we were dancing, the wet
patch wouldn't show … and, of course,
it didn't!

It didn't dry completely, but it did *begin*
to dry, and I danced every dance – not with
the comic, although we danced together
quite a lot. By the time the band played
'God Save the King', both Peg and I had had
a really good half-a-crown's worth!

As I drove by, fifty years or more on, with
my husband and daughter in a chauffeur-
driven limousine to be made a Doctor of
Literature for Services to Lancashire, I
thought well, it sort of evens things up
somehow.

So when I stood up at the graduation
ceremony to give the reply, in front of

Princess Alexandra, the four other honorary
graduates, and all the thousands of students
who had spent the last three years studying
for their hard-earned degrees, I told them
the story of the Lancaster and District
Co-op Annual Dinner and Dance.

Ever since my eightieth birthday, I've
been mulling things over – well, you do,
don't you? – and I've realized that I am one
of those lucky people who received a double
blessing from the Good Fairy when I was
born: first, to grow up in the North of
England, and second, to have had two of
the best and wisest parents in the world.
I sincerely believe that it was the things
I learned as a child that are the main reason
why I've had such a happy life.

Of course, at the time, I just took it for

granted. I thought everyone had a mother and father who loved them and taught them right from wrong. I now know, sadly, that this isn't so. I can hardly believe the things I read in the papers about child abuse, but once Scottie and I moved to London, we saw for ourselves the growing number of young people – no more than children, some of them – living rough, sleeping in boxes, and begging on the streets. What can their parents be thinking of? If you'd told my mother and father that in 1998 thousands of children all over Britain would be living on the streets in cardboard boxes, I know they wouldn't have believed you.

So my 'household tips' are reminders of the many proverbs that my generation and

I were brought up on, like all those 'copy-book headings' we used to have to write out in our exercise books. They taught us how to write neatly, and at the same time how to live a good and happy life. Some sophisticated people may laugh at the sayings in the Book of Proverbs in the Bible, but a world in which people lived by them would be a good world.

God knows, no one gets through life without a lot of sad things happening to them, or without doing and saying things they wish they hadn't. I know I haven't. But if you've had parents who loved and forgave you through all your early mistakes, and who helped you to cope with the trouble and sadness you experienced when you were young, it's like having a good map and compass to guide you through the rest of your life. The bracing common-sense of Lancashire folk – and there's still nothing wrong, that I know of, about calling a spade a spade – has kept me from a lot of vanity and folly long after Scottie and I moved South and made our home in London.

Since I first compiled this collection of little thoughts in 1993, my beloved Scottie has died, after 58 happy years of marriage. I miss him, and yet I still feel he is with me all the time; I talk to his photographs, or his favourite armchair, and I know he's still looking after me. He was my cog and wheels, and this little book is as much his as mine.

This book is a collection of the things I was taught as I was growing up in

Morecambe, and the things I've learned for myself over eighty years. I don't suppose they are going to shake the world – but who knows? They might make life that little bit happier for someone. After all, perhaps you know the old theatre proverb? 'If the show does well in Manchester – it will run in London.'

I dedicate it to our absent friend, the 'One Who Knows', and offer it with love and thanks to the great people of Lancashire, of whom I am proud to be one.

Thora Hird

July 1998

Neighbours

One of the things I love to remember about my mother was her great warmth and kindness to everyone, including all our neighbours in Cheapside, Morecambe.

Her door was always open, and people were in and out all day. 'Rat-a-tat-tat – Are you there, Mrs Hird?' They popped in to borrow things, to ask for advice, or just to chat and pass on the local news. If anyone

was ill, my mother would be the first to be
told, and would always call round to see if
there was anything they needed. She didn't
only offer her own services, either. We
children were part of what she had to offer,
and if there was a 'flu epidemic, my brother,
Nev, and I could expect to spend our days
scrubbing down front door steps, getting in
coal and shopping for the poor invalids all
down the street. I think we all sometimes
thought she was *too* kind! But the result of
it was that the whole neighbourhood was a
friendly, happy place.

Here are some of the rules my mother,
God bless her, always lived by:

☙ One of her favourite sayings was 'Well – they're not hurting anybody!' – a lovely expression that condones so many things …

☙ Always make the entrances to your home – front and back – welcoming, by keeping them swept clean and tidy. (Oh the *hours* I spent as a child, blackleading the coal-hole lid and rubbing our front door step with a yellow rubbing stone!)

☙ What a neighbour gets is never lost

☙ The Lord loves a cheerful giver

☙ Withhold from no one a favour when you have the power to grant it

- Keep your doors ever open to neighbours in need

- It's never too late to mend a broken fence

- But be sure not to remove your neighbour's landmark!

- You're always rich as long as you have a happy home, family, friends and neighbours

- Someone else's need is often greater than yours

And here are a few more ideas for life today:

♥ Support local events. The more people support them, the better they will become

♥ Share your skills with neighbours – you walk my dog, I'll wait in for your gas-repair man …

Forestall criticism

♥ If you move into a new neighbourhood, bringing with you a large noisy dog, teenage children with motorbikes and a small baby with a big voice – take the dog and kids round with you to all the nearby houses, shake everyone warmly by the hand, introduce yourself, your dog and your children by name, and say you hope they will help you by yelling at them when they become a nuisance

❧ Notice if neighbours' milk or newspapers aren't collected, or if curtains remain drawn all day; and keep a tactful eye on local elderly people and young children

❧ Support local shop-keepers and small businesses – you'll miss them if they have to close for lack of business – so give them yours

❧ Read the local newspaper and parish magazine, and send them ideas and articles of your own

❧ If you're throwing a party, invite the neighbours – you might even discover you like them!

❧ Tune in to your local radio station. Join in the 'Phone-Ins' about local matters

❧ Get to know the names of all the roads in your neighbourhood, and take an interest in local history and geography as well as current affairs

❧ If your neighbours belong to a different faith from yours, ask them what their feast days and holy days are, and give them a card or gift to commemorate them

- Ⓦ Get to know the Postman, Milkman, Paperboy and anyone else who delivers to your home – they will often be the local 'opinion formers'

- Ⓦ Have reciprocal arrangements with your neighbours – I don't complain about your noisy children, you don't shoot our cat

Love thy neighbour – even if he plays the trombone.

Jewish proverb

Friends and Visitors

As some of you may know, I've always been able to reel off the names of my best friends from school: Ada Lob, Mabel Bagshaw, Una Yates, Kathy Mortimer, Lilian Cross, Maudie Poles, Vera Muff, Madge Peel …
No, I'm not making them up – honestly!
We were all pupils at 'Miss Nelson's', the Preparatory School, Morecambe, in Union Street. Actually it goes even better when you

call them out like our school register – it's
as good as a story: Lob Ada, Muff Vera,
Cross Lilian, Hird Thora, Stretch Billy,
Peel Madge ...

When Scottie and I came to London after
the war, we found that people in the South
always seem to be on the move, so we've
constantly been making new friends all our
lives. But there's always been room in
our hearts for our old friends too, and
telephone calls, letters and Christmas cards
have continually flowed between our home
in a London mews and familiar Morecambe
addresses. Childhood friends belong to a
happy time, when we were all preparing
to become decent citizens of the world
together.

❦ Keep secrets. (I kept a friend's 'cross my heart and hope to die' secret for over forty years – but she says it's all right to 'tell' now: her 'periods' had started!)

❦ Stick by your friends. If you think they have made a mistake – you can tell them later, in private … (if you really think you must)

❦ Some companions are good only for idle talk, but a friend sticks closer than a brother

❦ A friend in need is a friend indeed

- ☺ Don't feel you have to offer solutions to your friends' problems … but always be ready to listen to them

- ☺ Laugh at your friends' jokes – even the ones you've heard before

- ☺ Never refuse home-made bread, cake or biscuits

- ☺ Short reckonings make long friends (that means, be a bit quick about returning books or anything else you might have borrowed!)

- ☺ If a friend asks for your 'honest opinion' – it's usually the last thing they want

☺ Check the lock on the loo door before visitors arrive

☺ Have confidence in your friends

☺ Never hang up the telephone on anyone

☺ Don't feel too guilty about having an occasional angry outburst behind your friend's back – it's better than hacking her to death with an axe

☺ If visitors arrive who like to sing loudly – leave a strategic tuning fork in the bathroom

☺ Don't expect your friends to be mind-readers

- ☙ Turn off the radio or television when friends call

- ☙ Don't make all the running in any friendship

- ☙ Forgive people quickly

- ☙ Keep in touch with your friends by letter and telephone, even when you don't see them for years

- ☙ When you are a guest in someone's home, don't sit around in silence waiting to be entertained

❀ Look out for things to admire in your friends' homes and gardens – and tell them

❀ Be generous with praise, and mean with criticism

❀ Don't *worry* about your friends – pray for them, and wish them well

❀ Don't steal their thunder

❀ Never invite anyone to stay for more than three days

❀ Never give a friend a present that suggests they need improvement

❧ Let them finish their stories

❧ Make a will, and leave small bequests as mementos to as many friends as possible

❧ If there's someone you instantly don't like – get to know them better. You may change your mind

❧ If there's someone you are instantly attracted to – get to know them better too. You may change your mind.

If our old friends could shed certain of their peculiarities, we should not like them.

Goethe

Family Love

My brother Neville was one of the
funniest people I have ever met. He made
everybody laugh. My mother would be
out washing down the front, and a
neighbour would pass and say 'Ee, Mrs
Hird, your Neville was talking to us the
other day – he-hee! Hee-hee! Hee-hee-hee-
hee-hee!' and they'd walk off still laughing –
without ever saying what he'd said! My

mother used to say to him 'Oh, You!'

To have a brother older than oneself, and one you love dearly, is one of life's blessings. I have often wished I'd been clever enough to produce an older brother for Jan – but it was not to be. Anyway, once she'd arrived, it was too late! My older sister Olga was knocked down by a motorbike on Morecambe promenade and killed. She was buried on her sixth birthday. It was something my mother could never completely get over – what mother could?

I think it is partly as a result of that, that we are all so emotional as a family when it comes to partings and reunions. My mother would never let us leave the house without a big hug and a kiss, and any separation longer than a day was accompanied by

loods of tears. Jan and I, and Jan and her
laughter Daisy, are just as bad. In fact,
Daisy won't let her mother drive her to the
airport any more, when she's on her way
to America, where she's at University –
they both get too grief-stricken! Scottie
pretended to be gruff and sensible, but
underneath he was as daft as the rest of us.
Does that sound barmy to you? I bet there's
many of you who are just as bad as us!

🕙 Always kiss and hug members of your
family whenever you are saying hello
or goodbye – you may never see them
again

🕙 Don't be charming to strangers – and
then snap and snarl at 'your own'

- You know the old saying 'familiarity breeds contempt'? Don't let it!

- Tell your children often how terrific they are

- Trust your partner and your children – and show them that you do

- Mark the 'Rites of Passage' in family life with plenty of parties

- Keep yourself up to date with other members of the family's work and hobbies

❧ When your partner comes home from work with a long tale of woe, listen carefully for who are the goodies and baddies in the story – then boo or cheer in the right places

❧ Notice and admire when a member of the family is wearing something new

❧ Plan surprises for people you love – even when they are grown up

❧ Make an occasion of their important events, like examinations, job interviews, driving tests, golf tournaments, garden openings …

❧ Be loyal

- Never walk out in the middle of an argument

- Remember anniversaries – sad as well as happy

- Don't want or expect your children to 'succeed' all the time

- Give everyone enough space

- Don't always ask the oldest child to be 'in charge' of the younger ones. Remember he or she is still a child too

ꙮ Don't let the youngest child become everybody's pet, or everybody's dogsbody. Remember he or she is growing up too

ꙮ 'Middle' children sometimes need a little extra patience and understanding

ꙮ Refrain from regularly detailing *all* your partner's shortcomings – an occasional pat on the back will be much appreciated … once they've got over the shock!

ꙮ Don't require other members of the family to be permanently cheerful – home is where you should be allowed to have a good sulk occasionally

☙ Keep talking to each other

☙ Better a dry crust shared with love than a feast in a house full of strife

> *The sum which two married people owe one another is incalculable. It is an infinite debt, which can only be discharged throughout eternity.*
>
> Goethe

House and Home

Housework used to be much, much harder and more time-consuming than it is today. I've described fully in my autobiography, *Scene and Hird*, how I was brought up to be a champion cleaner; just the passage and stairs alone were a three-act play in our house! The passage was covered with oilcloth, then with carpet, purposely narrow so as to leave a margin of oilcloth

about ten inches wide at each side. A strip
of brass held the oilcloth firmly together
with the carpet. This strip of brass had to
be polished, of course, and the margins of
oilcloth on each side of the passage were
also polished until they shone like glass.
They were referred to as 'the sides', and in
house-cleaning parlance you would be
questioned thus: 'Have you done the brass
and polished the sides?'

The first flight of stairs consisted of
fourteen treads, carpeted with a bordered
stair carpet held firmly in place by brass
stair rods, which, each week, Nev or I
unanchored from their harbour and
polished. Again, the carpet was narrower
in width than the stair treads, which meant
that after brushing the stair carpet with a

stiff carpet brush, there were still 'the sides' to do. The procedure was to wipe each side with a soft cloth wrung out in hot water, to which a drop of Izal had been added, wring the cloth out again, wipe as dry as possible, and then polish with wax. What a performance!

Until very recently I have always done all my own housework. And I'm convinced that part of what makes my memories of my childhood home so happy was that it was always so fresh and clean – to say nothing of artistic! My mother always had the bedrooms and staircase decorated in delicate shades of colour-wash – the forerunner of today's synthetic paint. She used to say that the curtains and bedspreads and furniture made the rooms fussy enough, and that plain walls looked so fresh and clean. They always did, too. The drawback was, it wasn't washable like today's miracle products, so consequently a bucket of colour-wash was often to be seen in our house!

The fireplace was the focal point of the living-room. It had a fairly high mantelpiece that was skirted with a Cornish frill made of the same material as the curtains and cushion covers. My mother was Champion of the Northern Union with a fourpenny Drummer Dye, and many's the time I have gone to school leaving a mauve Cornish frill, curtains and cushion covers and returned home to find them all rose pink! The moment she had seen us out of the house, the drill was: all down, all washed, all dyed, all dried, all ironed – all up! Fab!

It all takes about an eighth of the time to get the same results today – but they don't last any longer! Twenty minutes later I'm still thinking, as I did then, 'Now why did I bother to polish that floor?!'

- ☮ If you are lucky enough to have a fireplace (I wish we had one) it *is* 'worth the bother' of lighting it

- ☮ Be kind to your future self … Be honest – will you feel like washing up those dirty pans tomorrow morning any more than you do tonight?

❧ There is no such thing as 'too much cupboard space'

❧ Hang up a big cork board and pin up the best/latest family snapshots for everyone to see

❧ Have a big dictionary somewhere in the house – nobody's spelling is perfect

❧ A wipe with cold tea is good for giving windows a sparkle. The world outside looks far more promising through a bright, clean window

❧ If your home doesn't let in much sunlight, try having vases of fresh flowers instead of struggling to grow pot plants

🕊 Keep a thing for seven years, and you'll always find a use for it. (I've got things I've had for seventy years – and I'm still not parting with 'em!)

🕊 Some people are natural 'hoarders' (me!) and some are 'throwers away'. If two 'hoarders' marry – they'll soon be needing a bigger house

🕊 Keep a special drawer just for writing paper, cards, pens, stamps and envelopes. Everyone needs them at some time – no one can ever find them

🕊 Re-use envelopes and unwritten-on backs of letters and bills – save a rain forest or two

꙳ Always keep a pair of scissors hidden where no one else knows where they are – all the others will disappear

꙳ The more expensive the glass, the sooner someone will break one

꙳ If you're hoping I can advise you about odd socks that disappear inside washing machines – I can. The only possible explanation is that modern washing powders are so powerful, they turn one sock per wash into a tissue!

Mid pleasures and palaces though
 we may roam,
Be it never so humble, there's no place
 like home.

J. H. Payne

Take Care of Yourself

Scottie and I pinned up a notice above the stairs in the mews, so we saw it every time we clambered up: *'I grumbled when I had no shoes – until I met a man who had no feet.'*

It's been there for years, and it's still a great mind-jerker. Everyone is tempted to grumble sometimes, or gets a twinge of self-pity – especially, please believe me, when climbing a steep, narrow staircase with arthritic knees!

We all say 'Mustn't grumble', don't we? And we mustn't! There's always somebody worse off – and in today's world there are plenty who are worse off …

One of the Commandments is: 'Love thy neighbour as thyself' – and I was brought up to believe that in order to love your neighbour, you first have to learn to love yourself.

⊛ Keep your hair on! (But, oh boy! What they *charge* these days – to cut it off for you!)

⊛ A good name is more to be desired than great riches

❧ Never fight a generous impulse

❧ If you can't sleep – read!

❧ If you still can't sleep – get up and write a list. Put down all the things that are worrying you, and do something about one of them before going back to bed

❧ Keep your finger nails clean

❧ If you have a streaming cold, go to bed for at least a day

❧ Go regularly to the dentist – you only get one set of teeth, so take good care of them

- ✆ Get up as soon as you are awake

- ✆ Take exercise – enough to make you gently out of breath for half an hour a day

- ✆ Keep a diary

- ✆ Keep all personal letters, even from people you don't like – they are part of your life story

- ✆ Remember your dreams – they are trying to tell you something

- ✆ Keep practising any skills you may possess, whether it's playing the piano or throwing darts

⊛ A nap in the middle of the day can do you good. If you wake up in your pyjamas – it's morning. If you're in your clothes – it's time for tea

⊛ Don't argue with the police

⊛ Once you've found a pair of eyebrow tweezers that really work, keep them hidden in a safe place, and never let anyone else near them

⊛ Go to the cinema sometimes – don't always wait for the video

⊛ Go to the theatre once in a while

⊛ Don't belong to a gang

⊛ Don't put on a funny voice when you answer the telephone

⊛ Play and replay your favourite records and tapes – don't leave them gathering dust

⊛ Re-read your favourite books

⊛ Don't offer people a limp handshake

⊛ Don't pass up the chance to have a ride in a donkey cart

⊛ Resist the temptation to buy a boat

⊛ Vote

⊛ A glad heart makes a cheerful face

⒞ But don't smile *too* much

⒞ Don't be an old stick-in-the-mud

⒞ You must change in order to learn.
To be wise is to have changed often

⒞ Be as kind and patient with yourself as
you are with other people

⒞ Keep your watch a few minutes fast

⒞ Build a few castles in the air – but don't
move in!

⒞ Never forget how to 'play'

*First learn to love yourself, and then you
can love me.*
St Bernard of Clairvaux

Animals

I have already said that we are a softhearted family, but to tell the truth, and be more descriptive, I'll admit, where children and animals are concerned ... *we are DAFT* (and I don't care who knows it!!).

Jan had a hen called Bertha who was *very* broody. In fact, if you had sat her on a pile of egg-shaped stones in a box of straw, she would have been quite happy. Jan and

William had an old Victorian greenhouse, so for warmth she was nested in a warm corner of same, on twelve guinea fowl eggs. It was a pleasure to look at her, she was so very contented sitting there! In due course, eleven beautiful, little speckled chicks arrived on the scene, and Bertha was beside herself with pride and pleasure. Now here comes the 'DAFT' bit ... we would go into the greenhouse to look at Bertha and her chicks and say things like, for instance:

'Now then, who's a clever girl?' or 'Well now, what have you got there?' And she would look at us with such pride (as though she had laid the eggs, not just sat on 'em!) They really were a picture – little black, speckled dark grey treasures.

Scottie was really bonkers about them too. Bertha would walk them down to the back of our cottage and we would sit at the kitchen window and admire the way she would pull a long worm out of the ground and expertly cut it into small pieces with her beak, and then seem to tell them in her 'language' to take a piece in their little beaks. She would pick up a small prepared piece of worm, and drop it in front of a chick with little gentle clucks. Honestly! We were all delighted, but it was Bertha who showed most delight – she loved her beautiful adopted family.

One morning I saw Jan coming down the path from the old greenhouse with the dogs, and it dawned on me as she drew near, from the sadness on her face, that

omething had upset her. She came to the
cottage door and said very quietly, 'Can
you come a minute, Mummy?'

I went out and followed her back to the
greenhouse. As we neared the open door,
she looked back towards me and said in a
very little voice, 'Try not to be too shocked.'

Dear God, the greenhouse seemed full of
golden feathers, and no sign of dear, loving
Bertha any bigger than an Oxo cube ...
Over one side of what had been their cosy
nest, were nine little heads, and scattered
about the floor were nine little bodies, the
black spotted feathers moving pathetically
in the breeze. Sitting huddled together were
the only two little chicks left alive. A rotten
old mink had got through a top window
the only window in the old greenhouse left

open – two inches, for air) and murdered the magic family ... *not for food*, just for the joy of killing. What a sad family we were!

A few mornings later, Jan discovered that a fox had taken one of her geese. When I said to her 'Oh, Jan, it's like losing one of the family!' do you know what she said?

'Well, Mummy, I know the fox has a lair up in the hedges in the top meadows, and it's got some cubs, so it'll have stolen the goose for their food. I would steal food for my children if I had to and they were hungry ... it's not like the mink who slaughtered the chicks and Bertha, just for the joy of killing.' Do you wonder I love our daughter more each day?

❦ It says in the Book of Proverbs: A good man cares for his animals – wicked people are cruel

❦ However small your garden, leave part of it wild for creatures like voles and hedgehogs to hide in

❦ If you want hedgehogs to visit – put out water and tinned dog food in the late summer and autumn, when they need to store fat for the winter. Don't put out milk – they can't digest cow's milk, and may die

❦ Attract a variety of birds to your garden with wild bird-seed and a bowl of water on a bird-table, and hang out a net bag of peanuts, or half a coconut. (But stop feeding garden birds once winter is over, because they teach their babies to depend on your bird-table instead of learning to look for natural food)

❧ Every St George's Day, 23 April, look out for early house-martins and swallows to start arriving

❧ A milk bottle or narrow vase is not a suitable home for a goldfish – they need a big surface for air

❧ If you find an injured, wild bird or animal, leave it alone for at least an hour before interfering. It may recover without your help

☙ Get your next pet from an Animal Rescue Home

☙ Don't buy a dog if you are out all day

☙ Make sure that your own puppies go to good homes. (Goodness – anyone who wanted one of Tess's puppies had to pass their 'A' levels in dog-owning before Jan would let them have one of 'em!)

☙ People often take better care of pets they have had to pay for, than ones they are given

☙ The best way to praise God is to love and enjoy his creation

Animals are such agreeable friends – they ask no questions, they pass no criticisms.

T. S. Eliot

God

When people ask me, 'When did you find God?' I always say the same thing: 'I didn't have to – He's always been there.' And that's true – ever since I can remember.

Some of the 'words of wisdom' that follow were ones I've seen on 'Wayside pulpits' outside churches, as Scottie and I drove past. When I saw a good one I would shout out 'Stop!' and as he slammed on the brakes, Scottie would say, 'Thor! What is it now?'

Please believe me, I don't think of myself as an especially 'religious' person. Even when I was presenting *Praise Be!*, I never wanted to sound as though I was 'preaching' or doing the vicar's job for him. What I liked best about *Praise Be!* was reading the thousands of letters from people who have become almost like friends; and seeing the faces of the people when they are singing the hymns – all of which tell me that there are still hundreds, no, millions of people like me, who know that God loves and cares for us all.

That's what I think programmes like mine are for – not to make 'conversions' or to raise lots of money for an 'electronic church', but to reassure anyone who's feeling a bit anxious or lonely that they are not alone. There are still plenty of us who believe that 'God's in his heaven, All's right with the world!'

Just a few weeks ago, we were filming *Last of the Summer Wine*, out in the country, and the caravans for the dressing rooms and make-up were out in the fields. One of the make-up girls found a baby rabbit under one of the caravans. It was a tiny little thing. She picked it up, and it was trembling with fear, but it seemed to be completely lost, so she kept it. We were all as daft as people usually are about a baby animal, and were saying things like 'Oh, looook! The dear little thing! However did you find it?' – as if the last thing you'd expect to find in the middle of a field was a baby rabbit!

In the evening she took the rabbit back to her digs, and was wondering what to say to her landlady. But when she got there, one of the landlady's two little girls was crying. The landlady said, 'Her baby rabbit has just died, she's so upset.' Our make-up girl opened her handbag and said, 'Oh, well, look what I've just found!'

I think God did that.

ⓦ Have faith in God

ⓦ If your knees are knocking – kneel on 'em!

ⓦ Religion is a road to walk on, not a
   fortress to hide in

ʘ Count your blessings every morning

ʘ Count your blessings every evening

ʘ No one is so superior that they have no
   spiritual needs

ʘ What is missing from: CH - - CH?
   UR. (Get it? You are! Isn't it good, that?)

ʘ Going to church, if you haven't been
   before, can feel rather like gate-crashing
   a private function. Try and find
   someone else to go with you, so there
   are at least two of you standing up and
   sitting down in the wrong places!

❀ If you have a garden, allotment or window-box, take something along to your local church or chapel in the spring, for Easter, or in the autumn for the Harvest Thanksgiving Service

❀ Master Carpenter – needs joiners

❀ X-mas without Christ is just a Blank Holiday

❀ Tell your local minister, parish priest, vicar or Salvation Army captain that you and your neighbours would welcome carol singers at Christmas

ʕ *Welcome* those carol singers when they come, with hot punch and mince pies – even if your favourite programme has just come on television

ʕ Today's mighty oak is yesterday's little nut – that held its ground!

ʕ Seven days without God make one weak

ʕ Instead of worrying – pray

ʕ Don't be put off religion just because you don't like some people who are religious

ʕ Leave a regular space and time in your life for prayer and religious ceremony

ⓦ Don't only ask God to help you – also ask him to use you

ⓦ Listen to the voice of your conscience

ⓦ The more you listen to God, the more He'll talk to you

ⓦ Go on pilgrimage

Which religion you choose is not nearly as important as a fundamental faith in God.

Arthur Ashe (letter to his daughter)

Food

Christmas Eve was always magic at 6 Cheapside. The door was open for anyone to pop in and be wished a Merry Christmas whilst they drank a glass of 'you-name-it-we've-got-it!' Jobs were done during the evening before, to lighten the burdens of Christmas Day. The vegetables for dinner were washed and prepared, sage and onion stuffing and apple sauce were made, six

dozen mince pies were baked, fresh fruit
was arranged artistically in a rustic basket
and decorated with sprigs of holly, dishes of
nuts and raisins and boxes of dates and figs,
Turkish Delight and crystallized fruits were
allowed on top of the piano, and a large
fruit dish was ready to receive the contents
of the box of tangerines and the fresh
pineapple that Dad always used to bring
home, along with twelve new gramophone
records, every Christmas Eve, without fail!

The 'Royal Standback' fire would be
blazing brightly and the emery-papered
and blackleaded grate reflected the flames
as its contribution to the warm welcome
extended at Number 6. The aroma of
mincemeat, pastry, apple sauce etc., from
the back kitchen was mouth-watering! Add

to all this the smell of evergreens arranged behind each picture, above the big old clock on the wall, and along the mantelpiece, and the slight whiffs of alcohol and cigars as different friends popped in and lifted their elbows to wish you 'all you wished yourselves'. The only word you have to describe our living-kitchen on these occasions is ***Magic!***

I don't think many people of my generation suffered from anorexia – in fact I don't know of a single one. You had to eat up and 'not be so kysty' (Well, that's how you say it – but I don't know how you spell it. It means 'Clear your plate, and don't be leaving bits'). If any of us ever left anything, my mother would take on an expression of deep tragedy, and as she scraped the plate into the bin she'd be saying, 'Think of the starving Russians …' But with all the shortages of two World Wars, no one turned away from the prospect of a good meal – even a figure-conscious, aspiring young actress! For me, mealtimes are always associated with happy family occasions.

I never understood why Scottie, when he was on his own, would go to great trouble to cook himself a proper lunch – a pork chop and two vegetables, and a nice spot of gravy – only to eat it off the side, standing up in the kitchen! But fair's fair – *he* couldn't fathom why I, when I'm alone, always set a place at table, or at least a nice tray and cloth, before sitting down to a measly sandwich!

I enjoy going out to a nice restaurant, but best of all, I love to see friends sitting round our dining-room table, sharpening their wits while the mouth-watering smells emanating from the kitchen make everyone relaxed and cheerful.

The Gospels are full of stories of Jesus and his disciples and followers sharing meals together. There was that picnic for 5000 on the Galilean hillside; the wedding feast in Cana; family suppers with Mary, Martha and Lazarus at Bethany, and at Peter's mother-in-law's house in Capernaum; then there was at least one big, formal dinner party with Simon the Pharisee, and a spur-of-the-moment visit for a meal with Zacchaeus.

❦ A cup of coffee, a chocolate biscuit and a friend calling round for a chat – bliss!

🌀 Learn how to bake bread, or marry someone who can – just for the wonderful smell!

🌀 Drink plenty of water every day

🌀 Friends who have come for dinner will want to see you, and talk to you, not just eat – so don't make the dishes too complicated. You might even buy starters and pudding from a local delicatessen or pastry shop

🌀 Once in a while, on a cold winter's evening, gather round the fire with an old-fashioned toasting fork and a plate of muffins, and eat them 'til the butter is rolling down your chins

🐦 Fresh vegetables and fruit you've grown yourself have their own special magic you can't buy in any shop

🐦 Enough is as good as a feast

🐦 Never go on a diet – unless you want to keep putting on weight (*now* she tells me!)

🐦 Lots of little meals eaten through the day, each time you feel hunger pangs, are less fattening than stuffing yourself at one big spread

🕲 Freeze a few strawberries and raspberries each year, and have a 'taste of summer' one day when winter seems to be going on for ever

🕲 Eat slowly

🕲 Beware of sitting near a box of chocolates while watching television … it makes them disappear

🕲 If you are cooking for someone who is very tired or 'off' their food, prepare food that smells delicious while it's cooking (Scottie used to do this for me when I came home late from the theatre, usually feeling too tired to eat; the smell of his special dish of spaghetti, tomato

and onions bubbling away in the pan
soon had my mouth watering!)

ʗ 'Daily bread' is fuel – but occasionally
have a feast

ʗ If you want a feast for the gods, put
some crumbly Lancashire extra-strong
farmhouse cheese on an oven-warm
barmcake that has been liberally spread
with farm butter!

*In a sometimes lonely, somewhere hungry
world, for our friends and our food we
give you thanks, O Lord.*

Unitarian grace

Clothes

When my friends and I were teenagers,
we were quite unsophisticated by today's
standards, but we were all very fashion-
conscious, and managed to be quite smart.
In the autumn, for example, we usually got
our new winter coats (for best!) and the
comparing and admiring of each friend's
new outfit afforded us hours of pleasure.
As my mother always said, 'We weren't

hurting anybody!' But just occasionally, our
desire to be fashionable got the better of
our common sense. I had an Auntie Nellie
in Blackpool whom I was very fond of, and
sometimes used to stay with in the summer.
One Saturday, my best friend Peg and I
went over on the bus to see her. I have to
confess that our motives for visiting
Blackpool weren't just for the pleasure of
seeing Auntie – we also wanted to show off
our new, very up-to-the-minute patent
leather shoes with high heels, the smartest
things you can possibly imagine! It was a
sunny day, and after calling on Auntie
Nellie, Peg and I went out 'on the town'.
After giving the good folk of Blackpool the
chance to see and admire our fashionable
footwear, we went along to the pier, one of

our favourite spots, and by the time we got there, oh boy, were our feet 'feeling the pinch'!

Now there was a bit on Blackpool pier, near a little row of shops, where it was always cool and shady, and instead of wood, the floor was marble. I take full responsibility for what happened next. I said to Peg 'If we take our shoes off for a minute, we can cool our feet on the marble.' No sooner said than done, and with great relief we both took our shoes off and stood in our stockinged feet on the cool marble – and, as I'm sure you've already guessed, our feet instantly went 'shloop' and spread out like four pancakes! Neither of us could get back into our shoes. We tried swapping over – to see if I could get into hers, and she into mine – but it was hopeless! We were stranded like Cinderella's ugly sisters with the glass slipper!

Time was getting on, and we had to get our bus home. I draw a veil over the pathetic picture we made, our toes wedged into the front of our shoes, doing a sort of sliding two-step shuffle, desperately clutching on to each other and a few shreds of dignity, all the way back to the bus-stop.

♥ Only wear your smart, new shoes when you don't have far to walk!

♥ Get ahead – get a hat!

♥ Wear comfortable underwear, which fits properly

- ☺ If your clothes don't seem to fit any more, they must have shrunk!

- ☺ Don't drop your 'See-No' Hairnets on the floor

- ☺ Enjoy getting 'done up and dusted' once in a while

- ☺ You have to be very thin to look slim in loose, baggy clothes

- ☺ Be careful with horizontal stripes

- ☺ If you don't enjoy changing in and out of different clothes – don't become an actress

❦ However many clothes you decide to take on holiday – you'll only need half

❦ If you're over twenty-one – don't try on clothes in shops that have 'communal' changing rooms

❦ Keep shoes and leather handbags in soft bags or boxes – they'll last years longer

❦ Hang on to your favourite clothes, even after they are out of fashion. Your children and grandchildren will love them

❦ Teenage grand-daughters will always want to wear clothes you wouldn't want to be seen dead in

⊛ If you put on weight – buy bigger clothes

⊛ Don't pull down that wire coat hanger that's sticking out at the top of your wardrobe – there's five thousand others behind, all attached to it!

⊛ Men *do* make passes at girls who wear glasses

> *There's no such thing as 'bad' weather – only 'wrong' clothes.*
> Sigmund Freud

Men and Women

Don't get me wrong – I've never wanted to be anything other than a feminine woman! But there is one advantage men do have – and that is when it comes to (please excuse me) spending a penny. Scottie could have unzipped, been, zipped, and be ready to go … when I still hadn't reached my skinny knickers! And there's a mystery I'd love someone to solve for me. Why is it that whenever you visit the Ladies, you always find either a single sheet of paper, or a long trail of it on the cubicle floor? I always have to begin operations by detaching another piece of paper in order to pick up the paper on the floor (well, you can't be too careful, can you?) and deposit them both in the pan. But why is it there? Scottie assured me that he had never seen it in the Gents. I'd love someone to explain this to me.

For anyone who hasn't already read the story in my book *Scene and Hird*, I'll tell you how Scottie and I met and courted. (Of course, if you *have* read my autobiography, you can skip this next bit!)

When the Winter Gardens, Morecambe, was taken over by a group of wealthy northern businessmen in 1933, they transformed the old place. They gave it a face lift, an uplift, and every other kind of lift. A new orchestra, under the leadership of Cecil Hodgkinson, was installed in the band pit. I was invited to the opening night, a wonderful evening; everything gilt had been regilded, the entire place redecorated, the seats renewed, creating an atmosphere of opulence.

If I tell you that I didn't really notice the drummer in the orchestra, that would be a big fat lie. I did. But I didn't suddenly think 'My fate!' It was quite a few months before I started to think, '*Maybe* that's my fate!' by which time, you will have gathered, we were 'courting'. For three years we saw each other nearly every day, after which we became engaged. The 'proposal' took place by

moonlight on top of a little hill, known as
Woodhill, where Scottie and I often used
to go for a moonlight walk after work
(officially 'to get the theatre air out of our
lungs') – but what the heck, we were young
and in love.

Scottie had already brought up the
subject of marriage once or twice, but
although I knew he was the one destined
to be 'the one that *didn't* get away', I was
honestly not mad keen on getting married
too soon. I had a wonderful family life at
home, into which Scottie was warmly and
lovingly welcomed, and I loved him dearly,
so I said, 'I'll marry you if you'll have a little
house built for us on this hill!'

Two months later we were once again
walking on Woodhill, when I saw that the

foundations of a house had been dug. In the middle of the well of earth and clay, there was a small piece of wood stuck up. Nailed across it horizontally was a smaller piece of wood bearing the word, 'Sold', with the 'S' the wrong way round – which made it look a bit sad. I said to Scottie, 'Aw, what a shame! There you are, you see, someone has beaten us to it!'

Scottie put his arm round my shoulder and said, 'Did you ever think you would *have* to get married?'

'No I didn't!' I shot back, 'and what a thing to say!'

'Well,' he laughed, 'you'll have to marry me now, because this is *our* house!'

We had fifty-eight years together – and I wouldn't give a minute back of any of them. But, ooh! if only I could have had a pound for every time I heard him expostulate 'Thor! Whatever are you doing *now*?' – I'd be a rich woman!

ఴ You might as well accept it – you'll never understand members of the opposite sex

ఴ Choose your partner with great care

ఴ Never make all the running in a relationship

ఴ There is more to marriage than four bare legs in a bed

⊛ Pity is not a good reason for marrying someone

⊛ 'But I love him' is no reason for staying with a louse

⊛ A man with a glamorous girl on his arm always imagines people are thinking 'What a great guy he must be!' What they are really thinking is 'What's that beautiful girl doing with a jerk like that?'

⊛ Tall men fall for short girls, and short men adore tall girls

⊛ If you meet someone very attractive at a party and they say 'I'll call you' – they probably won't

⚘ Don't telephone them

⚘ There is no such thing as 'love at first sight'

⚘ Sex is a precious gift – never let yourself be seduced and then forgotten

⚘ Girls who play 'hard to get' get men chasing all the harder to get them

⚘ A lady never has to ask to be treated as one

⚘ 'The ladies' is not the plural of 'a lady'. It's what men call women who they think should wait on them

❦ 'The ladies, God bless 'em' make the tea;
women make babies, trouble, and hold
your hand in the hours of pain and
death

❦ Gentlemen – please adjust your dress
and *lower the seat* – before leaving!

❦ A 'gentleman' always gets out of his bath
before peeing (Scottie's contribution)

*Middle age is when you're sitting
at home on Saturday night and the
telephone rings – and you hope it isn't
for you.*

Ogden Nash

Work and Money

I don't wonder my generous parents never became rich. I once remarked to my mother, 'Oh, love, you are always giving, you'll never be rich, will you?' 'But we *are* rich,' she said. 'We've got you and Neville, and your dad and I have got each other, and look at all the friends we have!' She was right, of course. Nevertheless it has been one of my great regrets since she died, that success at work came too late for me to give her some of the things that might have made her life easier. But I know she knew we all loved her, and that was the main thing.

My first 'appearance' on the stage was when I was carried on at eight weeks old. My mother was the young heroine who had been 'done wrong' by the Squire's son, and I played the 'unfortunate result'. According to official records, I slept through the entire performance – and some might say I've been 'acting in my sleep' ever since. (But I hope they don't!) In spite of this auspicious start, and growing up next to the Royalty Theatre, Morecambe, where my father was manager for many years, I didn't immediately embark on an acting career after leaving school. I began by getting

experience in several different types of
work: assistant in a music shop; working at
my dad's office when he was manager of
Morecambe's Central Pier; draper's
assistant; cashier at the Co-op … And in
between all these, I attended night school.
On Mondays, I took French and cookery;
on Tuesdays, book-keeping, accounts
and English Grammar, on Wednesdays,
shorthand, and on Thursdays, typing. As
you can see, I wasn't relying solely on
making my way in the precarious business
known as 'The Theatrical Profession'.

Hecky plonk! Have you ever worked for
your dad? I'm only joking when I say that –
it was great really. But being late for work,
or late for anything, as far as my dad was
concerned, was the unforgivable sin. Mind

you, I admired him for it and it was wonderful training for us. He used to say that if you were late (let us for argument's sake, say one minute) you were as many minutes late as the number of people you had kept waiting for that one minute. Hence, once when I was one minute late for rehearsal when he was directing the Morecambe Warblers Amateur Operatic and Dramatic Society, he admonished me in front of everybody and said: 'There are sixty-three people here, and you're here, that's sixty-four. So that's sixty-four minutes you've wasted.' Red of face and very ashamed, I apologized to the whole cast. I was never late again – and to this day I have never been late for rehearsal. Anyone will tell you, I'm always one of the first, usually *the* first, to arrive. It's a good job, too, because I was married to a man as bad – or good – as my dad! If Scottie and I were going on a journey by train, he had the car at the front door so early that by the time we arrived at the station we could comfortably have caught the train prior to the one we'd gone for! But it all makes my working life run very smoothly.

- ✆ Don't be afraid to charge for your labour. My dad always used to say: If you work for nowt, you're worth nowt

- ✆ Don't procrastinate – Do it now! Tomorrow, today will be yesterday

- ✆ Be enthusiastic

❧ Don't try too hard to impress people

❧ They say it takes twenty years' hard work to make an overnight success

❧ Take pride in your own career

❧ A job well done is more fun than fun

❧ Think slowly – act quickly

❧ If something sounds too good to be true – it will be

❧ Most people like hard work – particularly when they are paying for it!

- Let people know what you stand for – and what you don't stand for

- Never let colleagues persuade you 'not to work so hard'

- It's not work that kills – but worry

- Little bits of money going out soon mount up – little bits of money coming in rarely amount to anything

- If you are very unhappy at work, you are probably in the wrong job

- Keep your shop – and your shop will keep you

❧ Don't judge every piece of work you do by the amount of money you make out of it

❧ In the morning, do the job you like least *first* – then you can enjoy doing all the tasks you like without it 'hanging over you'

❧ Be energetic

❧ If you work in an office – leave your work *in* the office

❧ Don't judge or criticize colleagues – and don't let them judge or criticize you

❧ Know your own worth

❦ Punctuality is the politeness of princes

❦ All is grist that comes to the mill

❦ A penny saved is a penny gained

❦ Don't be talked into buying things you don't want

❦ 'More expensive' doesn't always mean 'better'

❦ If you want to lose a friend – lend them money

Annual income twenty pounds, annual expenditure nineteen nineteen and six, result happiness. Annual income twenty pounds, annual expenditure twenty pounds ought and six, result misery.

Dickens (Mr Micawber)

Holidays

I'm no Freya Stark, but in our own small way, Scottie and I became experienced travellers. But no matter how far we've wandered, there always seems to have been someone from Lancashire there before us! We travelled round the world stopping first at Perth, Australia, years ago now, where I was appearing in Walter Greenwood's play *Saturday Night at the Crown*. I played the part of Ada Thorpe for the thousandth time on my second night's performance at the theatre in Perth. The very first morning we walked out of our hotel, a lady and gentleman walking along the pavement saw me, and with cries of 'Eeee, is it Thora?' approached me with affection. 'Ee-ee-ee, well!' the lady laughed. 'Now then! We never thought we'd see you in Australia, did we Dad?' Dad agreed. When I remarked that she sounded as though she might possibly come from Lancashire, she informed me with glee that a lot of the immigrants in Perth were 'from the North! In fact,' she assured me, 'most of 'em!' And she was right!

One of the many functions we attended in Perth was in the Assembly Rooms.

Everyone there was British and by the time we arrived after the show, the guests were well into the Saint Bernard's Waltz. As we approached the room by a long corridor, the MC spotted me – he rushed up to the orchestra waving his arms and silenced the lilting strains with a loud, 'Shurrup – she's here!' Everyone stopped dancing as though they were playing 'Statues', or as though it was a spot dance. I was bustled to the mike on the bandstand. I started to make a short speech, but there was something wrong with the mike (when isn't there?). So I said I would go to each table for a chat instead.

At one table I asked a lady, 'Are you happy here?' Like a shot from a gun, she exploded, 'I 'ate it! I've 'ated every minute

I've been here!' 'Oh dear, well never mind,'
I said, somewhat taken aback, 'perhaps
you'll be happier when you get more used
to it. How long have you been here?' She
gave me a piercing look as though *I* had
persuaded her to emigrate. 'Eighteen years!'
she exclaimed. 'And I've 'ated every bloody
minute!' I felt it was time I moved on to the
next table!

These days I very much enjoy going
on cruises with Saga, who organize
holidays especially for 'retired' people. It's
splendiferous! Sometimes Jan and her
husband, William, come with us, too, and
when we stop at a port they all go ashore
to explore, while I enjoy having the ship
practically to myself for a while, and settle
down to some writing.

Scottie and I both worked hard, so we both enjoyed and *needed* to get away once or twice a year. My one regret is that in spite of all this travelling, I've never managed to learn another language. If I had my time over, I *wouldn't* play noughts and crosses during the French class at night school. I did pass my French exam, but only because I was able to mime, 'Voici le tableau. Le tableau représente le grand-père, la grand-mère, le père, la mère, le fils, la fille et le bébé!'

Another expression my mother was very fond of was 'He's as nice a man as you'd meet on a day's march.' I used to say 'A day's march *where?*' And she'd say 'Anywhere!' But if you were marching along, you couldn't meet a nice fellow!

❦ Whatever you put out to take on holiday 'in case it rains' – leave it at home

❦ Always keep a torch and extra batteries in the car

❦ Pay attention at your foreign language evening classes

❦ Don't miss the chance of spending some time in a foreign country, on your own

❦ Travel light – there are shops 'abroad' too

❦ Always have an exciting paperback book in your handbag when travelling

- ☙ Don't leave your car at the airport – ask a friend or a mini-cab to take, and collect you

- ☙ Experience a 'souk' (an Arab market place). I'm mad on souks!

- ☙ Treat a very long flight (say to America or Australia) like a visit to hospital. Take a big bottle of water; take your shoes off; wrap yourself up in a blanket; set your watch to local time at your destination; get as comfortable as you can, and doze or sleep all the way

- ☙ Don't try to have a 'holiday' in a Third World country

✤ Arrange your transport 'at the other end' before leaving home

✤ Write a daily journal, or keep up your diary, while you are travelling

✤ At least once in your life, visit:
the gallery of the House of Commons,
the National Gallery, the Lake District,
Liverpool RC and Anglican Cathedrals,
York Minster, the Scottish Highlands,
the Isle of Skye, the Borders, the Norfolk
Broads, Boston Stump, Dublin, the
River Wye, the Rhondda valley, the
Pennines, Robin Hood's Bay, Covent
Garden Opera House, Blackpool,
Snowdonia, Beating the Retreat

🌀 Resist the temptation to buy a house when on holiday

Weary with toil, I haste me to my bed,
The dear repose for limbs with travel
*   tired;*
But then begins a journey in my head
To work my mind, when body's work's
*   expired.*

Shakespeare (Sonnets)

Getting On – Getting Old – Grandparents

I heard someone on the radio the other day, I wish I could remember who it was, saying that at forty-five she had just gone into the kitchen one day, to make herself a cup of tea, and when she came out she found she was sixty-eight! I know exactly what she means!

There is nothing in the world more surprising than discovering that *you* have grown old. I've sometimes found myself giving a talk, perhaps for 'Help the Aged', to a group of 'elderly people' and it will gradually dawn on me that I am probably the oldest person in the room! I don't feel any different inside from when I was a young woman. When I'm working I don't feel any of the aches or pains which, I must admit, I do sometimes experience these days, especially at night when I can't sleep. I always say a big 'thank you' to Him Upstairs for that, because of all the blessings of my life, still to be able to work is the one I'm most grateful for. When people say to me 'You should take it easier now. Why don't you stop doing so much?' I reply 'Why? Do you want me to die?' I know that not everyone of my age is lucky enough to be *able* to work.

Our two grandchildren are grown up now. It's over twenty years since I wrote my autobiography so that they would know about my childhood, and the world I grew up in, which seems so different from theirs today.

The world has changed – but their mother has taught them the same Christian values that we taught her.

❧ Take your children and grandchildren to see the place where you were born

❧ You're as young as you feel – a lot younger than you look!

❧ Don't get upset by what you read in the newspapers

❧ Tell your grandchildren about the 'olden days'

❧ Check your old list of 'things I want to do before I die' – and do them

❧ Don't assume you always know best

❧ Try to be stoical about your aches and pains – there's nothing anyone can do about them

❧ Remember, honestly, how you were when you were young

❧ Be brief!

❧ Go on a Saga holiday

❦ They *will* all have heard that story of yours before – but if you tell it *well* they won't mind hearing it again

❦ It sometimes takes as much generosity of spirit to *receive* help as to give it

❦ When in doubt, ask a young person. They know everything!

❦ Don't always expect younger people to wait on you

❦ Visit second-hand bookshops – you may find books there, like old friends, you had almost forgotten about

♥ Give away some of your treasures today to the people who will miss you tomorrow

♥ A wise grandparent doesn't give visiting grandchildren a drum or a trumpet for Christmas

♥ Write down, or speak into a cassette recorder, all your memories – they are 'living history'

♥ Face death with courage and serenity

♥ Re-read all the letters you've kept over the years – the wonderful thing is, you won't have to answer them!

☙ Remember – old age ain't for sissies

You know you're getting old when the
candles cost more than the cake!

Bob Hope

And one last word:

Remember – we don't stop doing things
because we have grown old – we grow old
because we have stopped doing things